P. J.'S
BAREFOOT
ALL OVER

Bil Keane

FAWCETT GOLD MEDAL • NEW YORK

A Fawcett Gold Medal Book
Published by Ballantine Books
Copyright © 1993 by Bil Keane, Inc.
Distributed by King Features Syndicate, Inc.

Library of Congress Catalog Card Number: 93-90193

ISBN 0-449-14811-4

Manufactured in the United States of America

First Edition: August 1993

"How old does PJ hafta be before
he's finally housebroken?"

"When we play Hide-and-Seek, PJ
always hides in the same place
and gets mad when I find him."

"Oh. I thought someone was
at the door."

"I wish we never had PJ!"

"Italics makes it look like
the wind's blowing."

"When I grow up will I still
look like me?"

"The computer and the
microwave are talkin'
to each other!"

"You behave back there or we're
turning this car around
right now!"

"My mom bought it and wrapped it.
I didn't KNOW it was a
comb and brush!"

"Why is Grandma's zip code different
from ours and we're in
the same family?"

"Mommy! I have something GLAD
to show you!"

"Daddy! Your compass is on 'empty'!"

"Go ask Mommy to comb your hair.
You've gotten it
all wrinkled."

"Can I be thankful without eatin'
sweet potatoes?"

"Grandmas aren't all alike. Ours
sews, Claire's golfs, and
Lori's rides a mo-ped."

"I sure wish Mother Nature would phone her plumber."

"Daddy wants to read the back
of that horsie you cut out
of his magazine."

"So far I've got, 'Dear Grandma.
I'm fine. How are you?'...What
else is there to say?"

" 'Bone' doesn't rhyme with 'none.' "

"I didn't eat my breakfast and
now I have a head-egg."

"Fingers like mittens better
'cause they don't get
lonely in them."

"Can I rain on the clothes
for you?"

"How can we be on the cutting edge
of something if Mommy won't let
us play with anything sharp?

"Barfy's a good watchdog, Mommy.
Look how he can watch TV."

"Wigglin' a loose tooth hurts,
but it hurts good."

"Mommy! The pot's throwing up!"

"Billy, did you forget something
last night?"

"I'm helpin' Daddy shovel
the path."

"'Stead of reindeer, Santa should
get some SNOWdeer!"

"Daddy captured a Christmas tree!"

"Wow! Morrie was born on December 24th! He just missed bein' Baby Jesus by that much!"

"Mommy, do you think Santa Claus
has a fax machine?"

"I'm in a school play, Mommy.
Will you help me learn
my line?"

"You can't sleep there unless
you're gift-wrapped."

"Shall I play for you, pa-rum-
pa-pum-pummm...?"

"Ida Know."
"Not Me!"

"Before you guys open your presents,
I want to take some..."

"It'll be interesting to hear them
tell THEIR children what they
had to do without."

"Billy knows my name is Jeffy, but
he keeps callin' me Roger."

"This fruitcake doesn't have
enough CAKE in it."

"You said the shaving cream I gave
you was just what you needed,
but you're not using it."

"She watched a cartoon where all the stuffed animals came alive."

"I'm not old enough to have coffee,
Grandma, but I can have
coffee CAKE."

"How do you pronounce this
word: RSVP?"

"Did the new year get
here all right?"

"If you take a picture of me with
Barfy, you can call it 'Beauty
and the Beast.'"

"Will you turn off your shaver,
Daddy? You're makin' the TV
go haywires."

"When an 'O' sticks its tongue
out it turns into a 'Q.'"

"Mommy! Come and watch
the bobsledders!"

"I'd like to watch TV, but
I don't dare."

"I'd be a lot better at maps
if some of these rivers
ran straight."

"LET GO!"

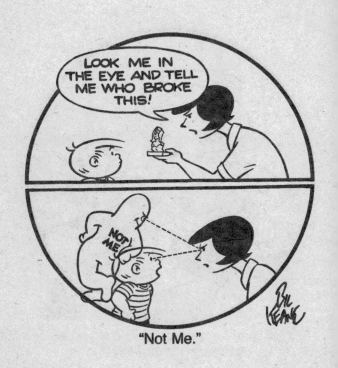

"Not Me."

"Oh boy! I'm gonna need my snow-
suit and ear mufflers!"

"I'm tellin', Billy! You shouldn't
even be JOKIN' about smokin'!"

"How 'bout trotting, Mommy?"

"The piano has no batteries, so I
can play it all I want."

"The hamsters need this door put
back on their cage, Daddy. And
watch where you're stepping."

"Michael J. Fox didn't grow up to
be big and tall, Michael Chang
didn't grow up to be big
and tall..."

"To FETCH a pail of water? Fetch
is what Barfy does!"

"I don't think half an inch is
enough to close the schools."

"Grandma, if you just pretend you're
nappin', then you don't hafta
go to sleep."

"Mommy, next time you buy crayons,
would you get a chestnut one?"

"Grandma was lucky. She got to
WALK to school."

"Mommy! Billy keeps makin' earthquakes!"

"It's real windy out
this morning!"

"I had my clothes hung up and now they're all hung down."

"You sure have gotten better lookin'
from the first time I met you."

"What do you get if you put a
quarter in this slot?"

"I wouldn't want to be a boxer.
They're not allowed to hug."

"When will it be my turn to listen
to Daddy's earmuffs?"

"They're called turnips 'cause we
turn up our noses at 'em."

"Someday my voice will be big and
I can be a real loud yeller
like Daddy!"

"I like soft things, like kittens,
marshmallows and
Grandma's lap."

"I don't think hair spray will
keep him from melting."

"I made a belt for you, Grandma.
I cut it out of Daddy's
leather jacket."

"Who teaches roosters to yell
'cock-a-doodle-doo'?"

"Theaters oughta have little tables
on the backs of seats
like airplanes."

"They put these strings around a
banana to hold it together."

"How did Mommy know I was eatin'
her chocolates? Did you tell,
tattletale? Did you?"

"Are you the curator of
this refrigerator?"

"Was Batman a batboy when
he was little?"

"Some soup comes out of cans, some
out of envelopes, but the best
kind comes out of the big
pot on the stove."

"This is the first sitting.
You're on the second."

"Who? No, I'm afraid you have
the wrong answer."

"I'd like to go to Australia.
It's my favorite color."

"Don't tilt
your plate."

"You can BUY Park Place, Dolly.
No hostile takeovers."

"Ahoy!"

"Billy's gonna show us how to
wash just ONE hand!"

"If he'd cut my hair slower I might finish a comic book."

"Barfy's tail would make a good
windshield wiper."

"Eat all your greens. It's
St. Patrick's Day."

"Grandma and President Bush's
mommy have the same
color hair."

"Kittycat better not see that.
It has cattails in it."

"Anyway, I can still beat you
at Nintendo."

"I think I'm gonna have some
more business for the
Tooth Fairy."

"Will somebody open the light
for me, please?"

"When we were in New York
did we see the Entire
State Building?"

"I'm gonna foam my runway!"

"If I ever build a house it's
gonna have nice WIDE
windowsills."

"If you can drink out of a fountain
by yourself it means you're
grown up."

"Why don't we just go over to the
gas station and let Mr. Bridwell
puff it up?"

"Mommy doesn't read us Ann
Landers, Grandma, just
the comics."

"Daddy said these yellow flowers
are for-Cynthia, but I grabbed
this bunch for you."

"Look! I'm pickin' my pizza up
by the handle!"

"Maybe you oughta put on your
high heels, Mommy!"

"How do ya like our house, Mommy?
It has a great view!"

"Don't worry — I'm gettin' every
last bit of it swept up and
put back in the box."

"Big deal. Grandma has that picture
on her calendar."

"Will these make my feet
hippity-hop?"

"The three kinds of eggs I like
are hard-boiled, soft-boiled
and scram-boiled."

"This may be Good Friday, but
Sunday's gonna be
even gooder."

"Mommy, where do they grow
jelly beans?"

"I forget. What was it you said I
shouldn't tell Grandma?"

"I found a dime, Mommy! Will you
take me to the mall?"

"Why's he wearin' his investments?"

"The Ferrells have a new three-
wheeler bike with a motor, but
it's for their grandfather."

"I'm gonna clean and dust my doll-
house, Mommy. Can I have a
cloth and some dust?"

"Time to get into your bedjamas."

"If babies don't come with direc-
tions, how do mommies know how
to work 'em?"

"Mommy, PJ's in the bathroom
calling you!"